THE STORY OF THE
CLEVELAND
INDIANS

SEC.
14
ROW
8
SEAT
10

Good This Ticket For FOURTH GAME

GRANDSTAND SEAT $6.00
Ext. Price $5.00 .- Tax $1.00 - TOTAL

GAME 4

Right hereby reserved to refund said price
and revoke license granted by this ticket.

Thomas Alspaugh
PRES.

DAY GAME
THE BALLPARK
★ ★
American League
vs.
National League

Thomas Alspaugh
PRES.

Read Important
Notices on
Reverse Side
★
Do Not Detach
This Coupon From
Rain Check

GAME 4

RAIN CHECK

DAY GAME
GRANDSTAND SEAT $6.00
Ext. Price $5.00
Fed. Tax $1.00
TOTAL

Right hereby reserved to refund said price and revoke
license granted by this ticket.

READ IMPORTANT NOTICES
ON REVERSE SIDE

Thomas Alspaugh
PRES.

SEC.
14
ROW
8
SEAT
10

GAME 4

Published by Creative Education
P.O. Box 227, Mankato, Minnesota 56002
Creative Education is an imprint of The Creative Company

Design and production by Blue Design
Printed in the United States of America

Photographs by Getty Images (AFP/AFP, Victor Baldizon/MLB Photos, KIMBERLY BARTH/AFP, Bruce Bennett Studios, Jonathan Daniel, Al Fenn//Time Life Pictures, Otto Greule Jr, Harry How, Yale Joel//Time Life Pictures, Kidwiler Collection/Diamond Images, Andy Lyons, Major League Baseball Photos/MLB, Jim McIsaac, MPI, National Baseball Hall of Fame Library/MLB Photos, Hy Peskin//Time Life Pictures, Photo File, Photo File/MLB Photos, Tom Pidgeon/Allsport, Rich Pilling/MLB Photos, TONY RANZE/AFP, Ron Vesely/MLB Photos, John Williamson/MLB Photos), Bryan Hunter

Library of Congress Cataloging-in-Publication Data

Pueschner, Gordon.
The story of the Cleveland Indians / by Gordon Pueschner.
p. cm. — (Baseball: the great American game)
Includes index.
ISBN-13: 978-1-58341-485-9
1. Cleveland Indians (Baseball team)—History—Juvenile literature. I. Title. II. Series.

GV875.C7P84 2007
796.357'640977132—dc22   2006027458

First Edition
9 8 7 6 5 4 3 2 1

Cover: Pitcher Bob Feller
Page 1: Shortstop Lou Boudreau
Page 3: Pitcher C.C. Sabathia

THE STORY OF THE
CLEVELAND INDIANS

by Gordon Pueschner

Cleveland Indians

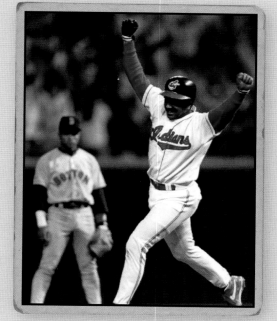

T he first game of the American League Division Series is dead-locked at 4–4. It's the bottom of the 13th inning, there are two outs and nobody on, and fans are beginning to wonder if the game will ever end. It seems that the Cleveland Indians, who have been waiting 47 years for a postseason win, may again be denied. But all doubts disappear when Indians catcher Tony Peña steps to the plate. He stands there, cocking his bat and waiting for the Boston Red Sox's Zane Smith to throw the perfect pitch. Smith finally does, and Peña is all over it, smacking the ball out of the park to give Cleveland a dramatic 5–4 win. The Indians will sweep the Sox to make it to the World Series, and although they will lose the championship after seven tough games, the 1995 season proved beyond a doubt that the Cleveland Indians were back.

INDIANS ORIGINS

Perched on the banks of Lake Erie, Cleveland, Ohio, has served as a crucial link for manufactured goods on their way to and from all parts of the world since the 1830s. Products from the Atlantic Ocean and the Great Lakes have been shipped down the Mississippi River to the Gulf of Mexico or loaded onto railroad cars for more than 150 years, providing a livelihood for many of the nearly three million people who live in the area.

The Cleveland Indians, often called "The Tribe," have a long history that stretches back to 1871, when the Cleveland Forest Citys were part of baseball's first professional league, the National Association. Cleveland's baseball team changed hands numerous times over the next 19 years, passed around to whatever league would have it. In 1890, the National League (NL) Cleveland Spiders acquired rookie pitcher Cy Young. The future Hall-of-Famer would spend the next eight years in his home state, perfecting the cyclonic pitch that would earn him more wins (511) and complete games (749) than any other pitcher in major-league history.

For Spiders fans from 1897 to 1899, one of the biggest attractions was outfielder Louis "Chief" Sockalexis, a Native American who was known for

CY YOUNG – When Young started his pro pitching career in 1890, the distance from the pitcher to home plate was a mere 50 feet rather than the 60.5 feet it is today. Young did farm work in the off-season to stay in shape and eventually won 511 games.

NAP LAJOIE

GREATEST BATTING RACE EVER

One of the most intriguing and controversial aspects of the 1910 season was the batting race between Cleveland second baseman Nap Lajoie and Detroit Tigers center fielder Ty Cobb. In 1910, Lajoie smacked the ball to every corner of the park, hitting well above .350 for most of the year. As the season wound down, he and Cobb were locked in a race for the AL batting title. To add some flavor to the race, the Chalmers Automobile Company promised a brand-new car to the winner. Cobb, believing that he had the race in the bag, sat out his final two games to preserve his average.

Lajoie, on the last day of the regular season, played in a double-header against the St. Louis Browns and got hits in eight of his nine at bats, bunting seven of those. The next day, some papers proclaimed Lajoie the winner, while others said that Cobb was. *The Sporting News* stated that Cobb had won, beating Lajoie .384944 to .384084, but the Chalmers Company was not as decisive; in the end, it gave both players a car. Ninety years later, it was determined that Cobb mistakenly got credit for two extra hits, but Major League Baseball refused to change the official record.

his brilliant base stealing and long, accurate throws from the outfield. But after compiling a 20–134 record in 1899 (the worst in pro baseball history), the Spiders were dropped from the NL. However, Cleveland wouldn't be without a team for long—the Cleveland Blues joined seven other franchises to form the American League (AL) in 1901. The following year, the Blues acquired two future Hall-of-Famers, second baseman Napoleon "Nap" Lajoie and pitcher Addie Joss. Joss, whose delivery looked much like a pinwheel spinning out of control, won 20 or more games four seasons in a row for Cleveland.

Lajoie also became known for his remarkable all-around skill. "Every play he made was executed so

ADDIE JOSS – Joss was one of the most respected figures in baseball in the first decade of the 20th century. Over 9 seasons, he finished 234 of the 260 games he started and fashioned an incredible 1.88 ERA. He died from lung disease at just 31 years old.

ADDIE JOSS

gracefully that it looked like it was the easiest thing in the world," remarked Pittsburgh Pirates infielder Tommy Leach. "He was a pleasure to play against, too, always laughing and joking. . . . You just had to like the guy." Cleveland liked the guy so much that the team changed its name to the "Naps" in 1903 and made Lajoie player/manager in 1905.

By 1908, Lajoie had the Naps battling the Detroit Tigers for the AL pennant. The race was a close one, but in the end, the Naps fell a half-game short of first place. Joss had greater success; he threw a perfect game against the Chicago White Sox on October 2, retiring all 27 batters in a row. "Joss sort of hid the ball on you," said St. Louis Browns shortstop Bobby Wallace. "One moment you'd be squinting at a long graceful windup, and the next instant, out of nowhere, the ball was hopping across the plate."

The Naps brought Cy Young back to Cleveland in 1909, and Lajoie returned his focus to hitting and fielding instead of managing. When legendary left fielder "Shoeless Joe" Jackson came on board a year later, the Naps seemed ready to contend again. But even the powerful bats of Lajoie and Jackson couldn't make up for what happened next. The team suffered two big losses in 1911 when Young retired and the 31-year-old Joss died suddenly of a bacterial disease called tubercular meningitis. The team continued to slide in the AL standings until 1914, when it finished in last place again and finally traded Lajoie away.

PITCHER · # BOB FELLER

This right-hander took the league by storm when he struck out 15 batters in his first major-league game on August 25, 1936, against the St. Louis Browns. "Rapid Robert" had a scorching fastball that was the standard to which all pitchers after him were held. He went on to play the rest of his career with the Indians, winning 20 or more games in a season six times, capturing seven AL strikeout titles, and leading the league four times in shutouts. Even though Feller's service in the U.S. Navy during World War II interrupted his baseball career, he remains the winningest pitcher in Cleveland's history.

BOB FELLER
PITCHER

CLEVELAND
INDIANS

STATS

Indians seasons: 1936–41, 1945–56

Height: 6-0

Weight: 185

- **266–162 career record**

- **1940 AL leader in wins, ERA, and-strikeouts**

- **8-time All-Star**

- **Baseball Hall of Fame inductee (1962)**

TRIS SPEAKER

ULTIMATE VICTORY

After Nap's departure, the team became the Cleveland Indians, but the name change didn't improve its poor performance on the field. It wasn't until the Indians signed center fielder Tris Speaker in 1916 that they began to see positive results. The fleet-footed Speaker made it hard for hitters to get a ball past him—he played so close to second base that he was more like a fifth infielder. "Tris played the shallowest center field I've seen," said Cleveland sportswriter Hal Lebovitz. "I seldom saw anyone hit the ball over his head."

Halfway through the 1919 season, Speaker was named player/manager and led the team to a second-place finish. Expectations were high for an even better year in 1920, but tragedy struck on August 16, when talented shortstop Ray Chapman was killed after taking a pitch to the head. Surprisingly, the downhearted Tribe rallied to win 24 of the last 31 games, capturing their first AL pennant. Cleveland faced the Brooklyn Dodgers in the World Series, and after four games, the teams were tied two games to two. In Game 5, the Indians quickly claimed the upper hand, winning 8–1. They didn't allow a single run in the next two games and went on to win their first World Series title.

Tris Speaker had a knack for hitting doubles, leading the AL in two-baggers in 6 of his 11 Indians seasons.

CATCHER · SANDY ALOMAR JR.

In his first season with the Indians in 1990, Sandy Alomar was named a Gold Glove winner, an All-Star, and only the third unanimous Rookie of the Year choice in major-league history. Seven years later, Alomar had a midseason 30-game hitting streak that fell just one game short of second baseman Nap Lajoie's club record, set in 1906. He also helped lead the Indians to a World Series appearance that year, hitting .367 with two home runs in the series. Sandy was the son of former California Angels All-Star second baseman Sandy Alomar Sr. and brother to big-league second baseman Roberto Alomar, a 12-time All-Star.

STATS

Indians seasons: 1990–2000

Height: 6-5

Weight: 235

- **1,233 career hits**
- **.311 World Series BA**
- **1990 AL Rookie of the Year**
- **6-time All-Star**

SANDY ALOMAR JR.
CATCHER

CLEVELAND
INDIANS

Indians fans were confident that pitcher Stan Coveleski's 23 wins in 1921 would boost their team to another AL pennant, but they were to be disappointed. For the rest of the 1920s, the Indians played well but never seriously contended for the pennant, finishing second to the mighty New York Yankees in 1922 and 1926.

Despite the team's lack of success, Cleveland fans remained loyal. In 1932, they were rewarded with the opening of the 78,000-capacity Municipal Stadium. On July 31, an overflowing crowd of 80,000 turned out to welcome the Indians to their new home. "When I went to the mound and looked around at the crowd, it was the most awesome thing I'd ever seen," recalled starter Mel Harder. "I mean, 80,000 fans. It was hard to believe so many people could be in one place." Unfortunately, the park wasn't fan-friendly—especially when

WORLD SERIES FIRSTS

In 1920, Tris Speaker's Cleveland Indians led the AL in triples, doubles, runs batted in (RBI), walks, and runs scored. Not only that, but pitcher Jim Bagby led the AL in wins, and Stan Coveleski boasted the most strikeouts. This loaded team faced the Brooklyn Dodgers in a best-of-nine World Series in October 1920. The Indians beat the Dodgers five games to two, with Coveleski winning three of those games. But most notable was the fifth game of the series. In the first inning, with the bases loaded, Indians outfielder Elmer Smith hit a grand slam (the first ever in World Series history). In the fourth, with two men on base, Bagby smacked a home run, becoming the first pitcher ever to hit a home run in a World Series. Then, in the fifth inning, with runners on first and second, Cleveland second baseman Bill Wambsganss caught a fly ball, stepped on the base to put out Dodgers second baseman Pete Kilduff, then tagged out catcher Otto Miller, who was running from first. It was the first—and still the only—unassisted triple play in the history of the World Series.

INDIANS

clouds of mosquitoes blew in off of Lake Erie. Municipal Stadium soon became a ghost town, and the Indians reverted to playing their daytime games at League Park.

Fans had something to take their minds off the stadium woes when Cleveland signed 17-year-old pitcher Bob Feller in 1936—for just $1 and an autographed baseball! "Rapid Robert" would live up to his nickname, using his blazing fastball to lead the AL in strikeouts seven times. Famed Chicago White Sox pitcher Ted Lyons once remarked, "It wasn't until you hit against him that you knew how fast he really was, until you saw with your own eyes that ball jumping at you."

Four years later, Rapid Robert was still going strong. On opening day of the 1940 season, Feller threw a no-hitter against the White Sox, and the Indians played tug-of-war for first place with the Detroit Tigers all year. After having a four-game lead demolished in early September, the team stumbled through the next few weeks to finish one game behind the Tigers. When the U.S. entered World War II the next year, many baseball players, including Feller, went off to fight in the war, stranding the Indians at the bottom of the AL.

THE BILL VEECK ERA

By the time the war ended in 1945, shortstop Lou Boudreau had become player/manager of the Indians. In 1946, Feller returned from the war and to top form, winning 26 games with 348 strikeouts, a club record. "I didn't know much," Feller later said humbly about himself. "I just reared back and let them go. Where the ball went was up to heaven."

Where Indians fans went, though, was up to new owner Bill Veeck. The

LOU BOUDREAU – Boudreau was a cornerstone of the Cleveland franchise in the 1940s. In 1944, he batted a league-high .327, and in 1948, he captured the AL MVP award. Although slow defensively, he wielded a sure glove and always seemed perfectly positioned.

LOU BOUDREAU

BILL VEECK

team may have finished in sixth place that year, but attendance topped one million for the first time, due to Veeck's attention-grabbing antics. He gave out prizes, shot off fireworks, and drove relief pitchers to the mound in a red jeep, among other things. Veeck continued his groundbreaking moves in 1947 by signing the second African American to ever play in the majors, center fielder Larry Doby, who would become a seven-time All-Star.

The next year, Bob Lemon, a sinkerball specialist, racked up 20 wins and helped the Indians squeak by the Boston Red Sox to claim the AL pennant.

FIRST BASEMAN · JIM THOME

Before Cleveland drafted him in 1989, Jim Thome grew up a Chicago Cubs fan in Peoria, Illinois, and was a two-sport star in baseball and basketball throughout high school and college. Thome hit his stride in 1995, when he bashed 25 home runs and batted .314. But that was only the beginning; in 1996, he hit 38 home runs. He just kept slugging away, hitting 49 in 2001 and 52 (a career high) in 2002. Because Thome's hitting success also translated into financial success, he was able to put all 10 of his nieces and nephews through college.

STATS

Indians seasons: 1991–2002

Height: 6-4

Weight: 220

- **1,302 career RBI**

- **472 career HR**

- **2003 AL leader in home runs (47)**

- **5-time All-Star**

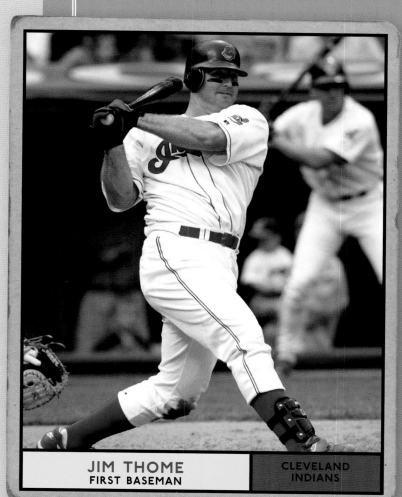

JIM THOME
FIRST BASEMAN

CLEVELAND
INDIANS

The Tribe faced the Boston Braves in a 1948 World Series that was all about pitching. In Game 1, Feller threw a two-hit game, but the Indians struggled at the plate and lost. Game 2 found the Tribe trailing the Braves again, so Boudreau sent Satchel Paige in to see what he could accomplish. Paige, fresh from the Negro Leagues, then became the first African American to pitch in a World Series. Unfortunately, his two-thirds of an inning was not impressive, and he was quickly replaced. The Indians pulled off a win in that game and the next two as well, putting them ahead three games to one. After the Braves won Game 5, Cleveland retaliated with a decisive 4–3 win in Game 6 to claim its first world championship since 1920.

The championship did not guarantee success for the following season, though. Cleveland's dive to third place prompted Veeck to sell the club, and in 1951, Boudreau was replaced as manager. The team responded well under new leadership, as the pitching staff led the way to 93 wins and third baseman Al Rosen, the reigning AL home run champion, drove in 102 runs. Despite such individual successes, the Indians finished in second place behind the New York Yankees for the first of three straight seasons.

Everything changed in 1954 when the Tribe won a league-record 111 games and finally finished ahead of New York. Indians fans were confident that the

DEADLOCKED

The Cleveland Indians had the makings of a remarkable team in 1948. Player/manager Lou Boudreau was named AL Most Valuable Player (MVP), pitcher Bob Feller led the league in strikeouts, and hurlers Bob Lemon and Gene Bearden each won 20 games. With such a collection of talent, it was no wonder that the Indians led the AL in batting average, earned run average (ERA), and fielding average. But Cleveland wasn't the league's only red-hot team; the Boston Red Sox remained neck and neck with Cleveland until the very end, when the two teams tied in a dead heat. A one-

game playoff was needed to decide the winner of the AL pennant, and the game was scheduled for October 4 in Boston's Fenway Park. In the first inning, Boudreau hit a home run, giving the Indians an early lead. But Boston responded quickly, tying the game. Things stayed deadlocked until the fourth, when Indians third baseman Ken Keltner smashed a three-run homer and outfielder Larry Doby scored on a sacrifice bunt, giving Cleveland a 5–1 lead. In the sixth, Boudreau hit another home run, and the Indians never looked back. They won the game 8–3, which sent them to their third World Series.

INDIANS

[21]

SECOND BASEMAN · NAP LAJOIE

Known for his easy smile and jokester personality, Nap Lajoie was well-liked by both teammates and opponents. Even though his batting stance appeared somewhat lazy, Nap worked tirelessly to become one of the best hitters in baseball. He hit over .300 in 16 of his 21 years in the big leagues and was such an incredible all-around player that Cleveland named the team after him for a while (1903–14). He led the league four times in hits and doubles, and so formidable was his reputation that, in one game, he became the first player ever to be intentionally walked with the bases loaded.

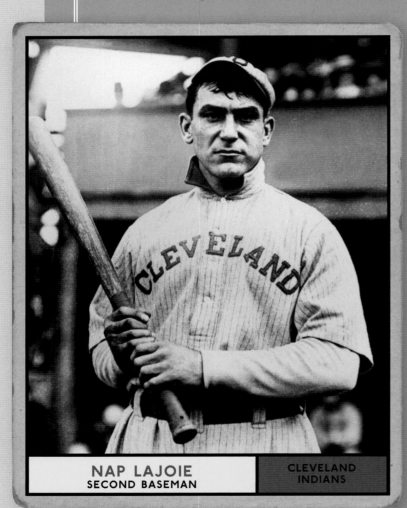

NAP LAJOIE
SECOND BASEMAN

CLEVELAND
INDIANS

STATS

Indians seasons: 1902–14

Height: 6-1

Weight: 195

- **1,599 career RBI**

- **.338 career BA**

- **1901 AL Triple Crown winner**

- **Baseball Hall of Fame inductee (1937)**

BOB LEMON

Bob Lemon started his Indians career at third base before finding pitching success with his great sinking fastball.

A BANNER SEASON

The 1953 season ended in frustration as the Indians finished second to the New York Yankees for the third year in a row. There was no indication that 1954 was going to be any different when the Indians were tied with the Yanks until April 30. Then, starting on May 15, the Tribe went on an 11-game winning streak and, by June, reached first place. In June and July, the Indians won 41 games, but the Yankees were hot on their trail, winning 43 of their own. New York stayed close until September, when the teams met for a double-header in Cleveland's Municipal Stadium. A record 84,587 fans turned out to see if the Indians could finally put their archenemy away. In the first game, Indians hurler Bob Lemon threw a six-hitter to win. The next game, pitcher Early Wynn outdid Lemon, throwing a three-hitter to blank the Yankees. In the end, the Indians closed the season with a league-record 111 wins, leaving the Yanks a full eight games behind. Although they eventually lost the World Series to the New York Giants, 1954 went down as a banner year for the Indians.

team would prove invincible as it faced the New York Giants in the World Series. Game 1 was a nail-biter, going to the bottom of the 10th inning before the Giants squeezed out a 5–2 victory. The stunned Indians never recovered, and the Giants went on to sweep all four games. Cleveland fans were also dazed; the only thing they could hope for was another shot the next year. But that opportunity didn't materialize. In fact, 41 years would pass before the Indians would make it back to postseason play.

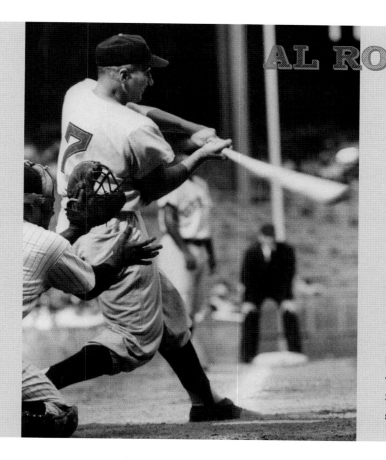

AL ROSEN

AL ROSEN – Nicknamed "Flip," Rosen was one of baseball's tough guys. Although the former boxer was inconsistent in the field, he was dynamite at the plate. He was the hero of the 1954 All-Star Game played in Cleveland, slugging two home runs.

ROCKY COLAVITO

ROCKY COLAVITO – "The Rock" won over Cleveland like few players ever had, to the extent that even his frequent slumps were quickly forgotten. Crowds swooned over his movie-star looks during warm-ups, then roared as he slugged one home run after another.

THE CURSE OF ROCKY COLAVITO

ight fielder Rocky Colavito joined the Indians in 1956. The 6-foot-3 kid from the Bronx belted more than 40 home runs in both 1958 and 1959, becoming the first Indians player to perform such a feat. His 42 homers in 1959 tied him with Washington Senators first baseman Harmon Killebrew for the AL lead. Colavito became an instant hometown favorite not only for his bat, but also for the marathon autograph sessions he held after each game.

With Colavito's popularity on the rise, 1960 seemed full of promise for the Indians. But before the season started, general manager Frank "Trader" Lane made an unlucky deal in trading the beloved Colavito to the Detroit Tigers. The Indians dropped to fourth place that year and would take more than 30 years to recover from what some called "the curse of Rocky Colavito."

Throughout the 1960s and '70s, the Tribe seemed to keep giving away their best players for little in return—except in the case of star pitcher Sam McDowell, who won five AL strikeout titles from 1965 to 1970. In 1965 alone, "Sudden Sam" struck out 325 batters and posted an ERA of 2.18. He won a personal-best 20 games in 1970, but the Indians fell into a slump and traded

THIRD BASEMAN · AL ROSEN

A former amateur boxer who broke his nose 11 times, Al Rosen spent his entire 9-year career with the Indians. In his first full season (1950), he hit a league-leading 37 home runs, which was an AL record for rookies at the time. In 1953, he hit 43 home runs and collected 145 RBI but was one hit shy of having the AL's best batting average, narrowly missing the Triple Crown (as the league leader in all three categories). After he retired from baseball, he went on to become a stockbroker and then general manager of three major-league teams.

AL ROSEN
THIRD BASEMAN

CLEVELAND
INDIANS

STATS

Indians seasons: 1947–56

Height: 5-10

Weight: 180

- **1953 AL MVP**
- **4-time All-Star**
- **5 seasons of 100-plus RBI**
- **2-time AL leader in HR**

him a year later for future Cy Young Award winner Gaylord Perry. Perry's illegal spitballs were notorious—but generally overlooked by officials—and he used his special technique to win a career-high 24 games in 1972.

The string of talented pitchers in Cleveland continued in 1980 with Len Barker. He won 19 games that year, the most memorable of which was on May 15 against the Toronto Blue Jays. That day, Barker became the 12th hurler in major-league history to throw a perfect game. Unfortunately, one perfect game wasn't enough to put the Indians on a winning track. For the next five years, in fact, the Indians never finished above sixth place in the AL Eastern Division. Despite the continued losing streak, in 1986, the Indians attracted large crowds to watch outfielder Joe Carter drive in 121 runs and smack 29 home runs. Carter was the team's most exciting asset for the rest of the '80s, but in 1989, he was traded. When speedy center fielder Kenny Lofton joined the team in 1992, fans hoped that the Indians' trading days were over—and that their winning days had finally begun.

INDIANS

JOE CARTER

Joe Carter made headlines in 1987 by joining baseball's "30-30" club, posting 32 homers and 31 stolen bases.

SHORTSTOP · OMAR VIZQUEL

For almost 20 years, Omar Vizquel used his ability to seamlessly turn double plays and catch ground balls barehanded to put out frustrated batters. He once tied a record set by Baltimore Orioles great Cal Ripkin Jr. by going 95 games without committing an error. In 2002, he made only 7 errors in 150 games, yet the Gold Glove award for outstanding defense went to another shortstop, the Texas Rangers' Alex Rodriguez. Vizquel was the perfect number-two batter, an unselfish switch hitter who in 2004 led the AL with 20 sacrifice bunts.

STATS

Indians seasons: 1994–2004

Height: 5-9

Weight: 165

- **.276 career BA**

- **.984 career fielding percentage**

- **3-time All-Star**

- **11-time Gold Glove winner**

OMAR VIZQUEL
SHORTSTOP

CLEVELAND INDIANS

THE COMEBACK TRIBE

s the Indians were about to begin the 1993 season, pitchers Steve Olin and Tim Crews were killed in a boating accident. Just as had happened in 1920, the incident cast a dark shadow over a promising team, and the Indians struggled to keep themselves on track. But when they moved into a new stadium, Jacobs Field, and into a new division, the AL Central, in 1994, the future seemed brighter. All hopes were dashed by a players' strike, though, which started on August 12 and wiped out the rest of the season.

After the strike ended in 1995, the Tribe was finally given a chance to shine. That year, they fought their way to the best record in the league and clinched the AL Central by an incredible 30 games. Designated hitter Albert Belle led Cleveland's offense, becoming the first player in major-league history to hit more than 50 home runs and 50 doubles in a season, and Lofton led the league in stolen bases for the fourth year in a row.

The Tribe swept the Red Sox in the first round of the playoffs. Then they battled the Seattle Mariners in the AL Championship Series (ALCS), winning the series four games to two. After 41 years, the Cleveland Indians had finally returned to the World Series, and they were determined to show the Atlanta Braves who was boss. The series was a tight one, with five of the six

LEFT FIELDER · JOE JACKSON

Before arriving in Cleveland, Joe Jackson was a South Carolina mill worker who couldn't read or write. But he could play baseball. While working at the mill, Jackson had acquired the nickname "Shoeless Joe" for playing a game in his socks because a new pair of shoes had given him blisters the day before. In his first full season with the Cleveland Naps, the hardworking rookie hit .408. For his involvement in the Chicago "Black Sox" gambling scandal of the 1919 World Series, Shoeless Joe was banned for life from professional ball, but he continued to play in semipro leagues throughout the South.

JOE JACKSON
LEFT FIELDER

CLEVELAND INDIANS

STATS

Indians seasons: 1910–15

Height: 6-1

Weight: 200

- 3-time AL leader in triples
- .356 career BA
- .345 career World Series BA
- 785 career RBI

HOME SWEET HOME

Over the past 100 years, the Cleveland Indians
have called three unique ballparks home.
The first, League Park, was built in 1891 and
eventually had a capacity of 20,000. Because
the field had to fit into a cramped city grid, it
had some unusual dimensions. The right-field
line was only 290 feet from home plate, but for
players to hit a home run, the ball had to get over
a 60-foot wall—that's 23 feet taller than Boston's
infamous "Green Monster" in Fenway Park! The
second field, Municipal Stadium, opened in 1931
and could house up to 78,000. It was dubbed
"The Mistake by the Lake" by fans because of
its size and the horribly strong winds that blew
in off of Lake Erie. The center-field stands were
480 feet away, and no player ever hit a home
run that far. Indians owner Bill Veeck sometimes
moved Municipal's outfield fence 15 feet in or
out, depending on how it would favor the Indians.
The team's third home, Jacobs Field, opened in
1994 at about half the size of the old Municipal
Stadium, but it featured the largest freestanding
scoreboard in the United States and one of the
largest video screens in the world.

CENTER FIELDER · TRIS SPEAKER

The second player ever to win the AL MVP award (after Detroit Tigers great Ty Cobb), Tris Speaker proved time and again that he was one of the greatest center fielders of his day. His unique style of playing a shallow center field allowed him to make 448 outfield assists and to turn 139 double plays throughout his career. He led the league eight times in hitting doubles, and he assembled three hitting streaks of 20 or more games in a single season (1912). Named player/manager in 1919, Speaker led the Indians to a World Series title in 1920.

STATS

Indians seasons: 1916–26

Height: 5-11

Weight: 193

- **1,881 career runs scored**

- **.345 career BA**

- **792 career doubles**

- **Baseball Hall of Fame inductee (1937)**

TRIS SPEAKER
CENTER FIELDER

CLEVELAND
INDIANS

games being decided by one run. But in the end, Atlanta's superior pitching prevailed, and the Indians returned home empty-handed.

The Indians' fans gladly welcomed them back, and support for the team only increased the next year; tickets for the entire 1996 season sold out before opening day. The Tribe didn't disappoint their loyal following, storming to 99 victories to clinch the best record in the AL. But in the first-round divisional playoffs, the Cleveland faithful were shocked when the Baltimore Orioles beat the Indians in four games.

To make another run for the pennant in 1997, the Indians decided to get another power hitter. They traded the base-stealing Lofton for slugging outfielder David Justice. The change seemed to be for the best, as Justice hit .329

DAVID JUSTICE — Few players of the modern era became as familiar with the playoffs as Justice. Over the course of a 14-year career, he made it to the postseason 10 times (with 4 different teams). In his three full Indians seasons, he averaged 25 homers a year.

JIM THOME

JIM THOME – Thome was a feast-or-famine hitter, setting a team record with 171 strikeouts in 1999 but also hitting 33 round-trippers and drawing an AL-high 127 walks. Although never a star fielder, his defense improved as his career went along.

and slugged 33 dingers that year. The Tribe won the AL Central again, then defeated the Orioles and Yankees in the playoffs to make their second World Series appearance in three years.

The Indians faced the five-year-old Florida Marlins in what turned out to be one of the most dramatic World Series of the '90s. After six games, the series was tied three games to three, and everything came down to Game 7. In the bottom of the 11th, Marlins shortstop Edgar Renteria drove in the winning run, crushing Cleveland's hopes of its first World Series championship since 1948. "About a year and a half or so after that World Series," Indians manager Mike Hargrove later said, "a guy asked me how long it took me to get over that last game. I told him, 'As soon as it happens, I'll let you know.'"

HOPE FOR THE FUTURE

espite the World Series loss, the Indians were ready to strike again in 1998. They reacquired Kenny Lofton and again captured the division, meeting the Red Sox in the AL Division Series (ALDS) and swiftly taking a two-games-to-one lead. In Game 4, with the Tribe down 1–0 in the eighth inning, Justice swatted a two-run double, which was all the Indians needed to win the series. Next, they met the Yankees in the ALCS. Although Cleveland won

TRAVIS HAFNER

Travis Hafner joined the Indians in 2003 and earned league-wide attention in 2006 by driving in 117 runs.

only two of the six games, the team took some measure of pride in being the only team that year to win any postseason games against the eventual world champion Yankees.

Right fielder Manny Ramirez led the Tribe in 1999, collecting a club record 165 RBI. "Manny does everything so effortlessly, and the ball just jumps off his bat. He has the talent to hit a pitch no matter where the pitcher throws it," said Hargrove. The Indians posted a 97–65 record that season and clinched their fifth consecutive division title, becoming only the third team in major-league history to do so. But it didn't matter in the end; the Red Sox topped the Indians in the first round of the playoffs.

In 2001, first baseman Jim Thome smacked the ball all around Jacobs Field, hitting 49 home runs, the most in club history for a left-handed hitter. Another lefty, 21-year-old pitcher C.C. Sabathia, won a team-high 17 games and helped take the Indians back to the postseason. This time, the Tribe faced the Seattle Mariners in the playoffs, but even their 17-run explosion in Game 3 couldn't prevent their losing the series three games to two.

In 2002, the Indians fell below .500 for the first time in eight years. The next year, Cleveland reorganized and named former Boston Red Sox designated hitter Eric Wedge its new manager.

RIGHT FIELDER · MANNY RAMIREZ

Originally from Santo Domingo, Dominican Republic, Ramirez spent his teenage years in New York City, only a short distance from Yankee Stadium. Widely regarded as one of the most versatile hitters in the league, the powerful outfielder hit against right-handed and left-handed pitchers with equal success. During his Indians career, he collected 236 home runs and 804 RBI. He posted a career-high 165 RBI in 1999—the highest total in the majors since 1938. He also became the first player since Boston's Ted Williams in 1949 to have more RBI in a season than games played.

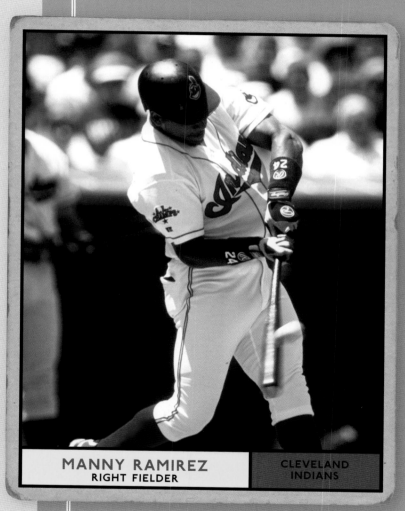

MANNY RAMIREZ
RIGHT FIELDER

CLEVELAND INDIANS

STATS

Indians seasons: 1993–2000

Height: 6-0

Weight: 200

- **20 career grand slams**
- **1,516 career RBI**
- **2004 World Series MVP**
- **10-time All-Star**

INDIANS

[43]

MANAGER · LOU BOUDREAU

At age 24, Boudreau became the youngest player ever to manage a major-league team for an entire season. In his first six years, his inexperience showed, as the Tribe never placed higher than third. Club owners weren't impressed. In 1945, they tried to replace him, but Cleveland fans protested so much that they kept him on. It was a good thing they did; a few years later, he led the Indians to a World Series title. Before becoming their manager, Boudreau was an excellent shortstop for the Indians and one of the league's top fielders in the 1940s.

STATS

Indians seasons as manager: 1942–50

Height: 5-11

Weight: 185

Managerial Record: 1,162–1,224

World Series Championship: 1948

LOU BOUDREAU
MANAGER

CLEVELAND
INDIANS

ALBERT BELLE

CONTENDERS ONCE AGAIN

In 1995, after the strike was over, the Indians put together one of their most impressive seasons ever, winning their first AL pennant since 1954. Indians pitchers led the league with the lowest team ERA, and outfielder Albert Belle became the first major-league player to collect 100 extra-base hits since 1948. In the divisional playoffs against the Boston Red Sox, the first game was not decided until the bottom of the 13th inning, when Indians catcher Tony Peña slammed a home run and gave the Tribe an appetite for more postseason victories. They took the rest of the series and went on to beat the Seattle Mariners in the ALCS, propelling them into the World Series. In the first two games against the Atlanta Braves in the "Fall Classic," the Indians lost by one run. Game 3 was at home in Jacobs Field, and designated hitter Eddie Murray slapped a game-winning single to give Cleveland its first win in a World Series game in 47 years. Although the Indians eventually lost the World Series, just being there was an accomplishment for a team that had suffered one of the longest playoff droughts in league history.

INDIANS

JAKE WESTBROOK

Wedge's no-nonsense approach and ability to develop young players started moving the Indians in the right direction. In 2004, they went 80–82, and in 2005 they improved to 93–69 and almost won the AL Central. Many experts picked the fast-rising Tribe to finish atop the division in 2006, but Cleveland struggled to a losing record. Despite the baffling step backward, the Cleveland faithful were confident that their club would be in playoff contention again soon. Besides Sabathia, the team boasted such talented players as switch-hitting catcher Victor Martinez, speedy outfielder Grady Sizemore, slugging designated hitter Travis Hafner, and pitcher Jake Westbrook. "We're strong, we're confident, and we've got some good ballplayers here," said Wedge.

Even though the long history of the Cleveland Indians hasn't always been a successful one, in their recent past, they have been among baseball's most consistently competitive teams. As fans of the Tribe now put their hopes in such heroes as C.C. Sabathia and Travis Hafner, hopes are high that the Indians will soon manufacture another pennant for the city by the lake.

Jake Westbrook bolstered the Indians' pitching rotation by posting 15-win seasons in both 2005 and 2006.